Poster Girl

A compilation of thought provoking posts

post·er girl

noun

a woman who epitomizes or
represents a specified quality or cause.

Dedication

Dedicated to my faithful followers and fans...
Those who see my posts like proverbs or psalms...
Seeking out my statuses...
for sanity and spiritual stability,
for humor, healing and hope...
I pray you feel and find the GOoD
in my personal reflections

Shout out to...

Every failed relationship,
Every missed opportunity, Every mistake,
Every lonely night, Every tear,
Every bit of karma that collected...

You taught me every lesson listed.

Table Of Contents

The Make Up

Greatness (poem)..1-5

Walk In Your Calling 6

Shrinkage 7

Anti Struggles 8

An Inside Job... 9

Shrinkage Continued 10

Focus 11

Survivor 12

O-Fences 13

Watch me work(poem) 14-18

Comprehension Levels............................... 19

Organically Weird 20

No Duplicates 21

Put up.. 22

Unlimited Plan.. 23

Pee Pee Premonition 24

INTIMID8TING (poem) 25-29

Unapologetically Intimid8ting 30-31

You Know You Knew................................. 32

Walls 33

Spiritual Stacks... 34

Can I Get a Refill 35

GPS.. 36

Trap Anointing 37-38

Reflections..39-48

What She's Wearing

Teach Me How To Give Up (poem) 50-54

Laundry or Lesson 55-56

Simone's Scripture 57

The Gift of Ghosting 58

Cheat Sheet Freaks 59

Fake Love 60

Accountability 61-62

Know Your Role 63

Cellular Man (poem) 64-66

Clear Water 67

Prepare A Place For Me 68

Worthy 69

A Fathers Affirmation 70

Mama's Gift 71

Worth It 72

Cape Off 73

Loveless Self 74

Reflections 75-82

The Height Of Her Heel-ing

Journey To Self Love (poem) 84-88

Self-Surgery 89

Still Bleeding 90

Pain Pals 91

Closure 92

Forgive Yourself..98

Liquid Love..99

Protect Your Spirit..100

Remy Riyah... 101-102

Random Thoughts On Sex...................... 103-104

Survivor (poem) 105-106

Still Fly 107

Got Light?...108

Spiritual Baths..109

Fall Fasting 110

Affirmative Prayer................................. 111-112

Decide...113

Letting Go...114

Open Up..115

Empathy, Faith and Optimism vs

Self-Love and Intuition 116-117

Keep The Change..118

I Feel Good (poem)................................ 116-120

Reflections.. 121-128

The Make Up

Greatness

Greatness used to haunt me.
I used to be so much of a coward
my own power used to punk me.
I always had a relationship with God
but most religions only seemed
to keep me convicted.
I always had respect for my peers
but their opinions only seemed to
keep me restricted,
like crank callers.
And if money was guilt,
and self doubt was some clout,
I would have been a well known baller!
A ball of confusion.
Confusing who they saw me as,
with who I was becoming.
I could always see all I could be,
but all they could see,
was everything that I wasn't.
Might as well had locked me in the pen.
They put a lock on my pen.
They saw I had a gift,
and automatically tried to box me in,
with a label.
But I told them,
'I ain't nobody's maid or mabel,
I'm more like a model,
and I'm gone run my runway my way,
starting today!"
I'm finding and redefining my God.
Getting into my odd,

1

even when the odds are against me.
Can't be fenced in.
I'm ok with not fitting in,
Cuz you can't be outstanding,
when you're too afraid to stand out.
I'm cut from a different cloth,
God quit making when he put my brand out,
 a whole nother fabric,
wreaking havoc on these haters.
Finally doing me,
like a habitual masterbator...
and I'm coming...
Full circle.
My crown chakra,
Royal purple.
I'm a queen secure in her queendom,
Securing her queendom.
A Goddess who always had it but just got it,
I finally know who God is.
So I'm capturing capabilities,
like the ability to move the souls of foes
who swear to God they aln't feeling me.
I've been through 12 car crashes
with no scratches, no scars,
Ain't no killing me!
Not my will,
It be the Most High,
So I don't live like most lives.
I don't think like most minds.
You can't see my vision with closed eyes.
I'm purpose driven so me quiting,
You can hang that up like a clothesline!

I'm on mine.
I'm gaining ground like
I just closed on some property.
I'm prospering!
Don't even call me K-Love...
Call me prosperous!
A profiting prophetess.
And my growth be my gross income.
I'm coming into my own.
I'm enlarging my territory.
And since the land's mine,
I treat them naysayers like land mines,
I blow up every time I cross one.
Lost ones.
Hoping to see me fall like Niagra,
But I go hard like Viagra!
I got a lil soul in my swagger,
so I'm stepping to new levels
like I got stilts in my stilettos.
Let's go!
I used to be afraid of greatness,
but now I'm stalking it!
There's a difference between speaking in faith,
 and talking sh*t.
Running from it and walking in it!
And I can't turn back,
can't turn my back.
I'm taking my turn back.
Once unequipped for the battle,
now I'm strapped like sandals.
Grabbing life by the handles,
and I can handle it.

I got a pocket full of hope,
and a purse full of purpose to gamble with
and I'm feeling lucky tonight.
I'm loving my life.
Living my dream.
So you can either dream with me,
Or sit on the sidelines and watch it.
Sit on the sidelines and knock it.
but my faith
will beat the breaks
off of anybody's logic!
You can't ration my passion.
You can't teach my tenacity.
So ain't no sense in even asking me.
You couldn't answer my calling
even if I gave you my phone.
World's best GPS couldn't put you on the path that I'm on.
So while you stay second guessing,
I go different directions,
Cuz I was given different directions!
I could feel it in my midsection.
I was flirting with my purpose and got pregnant with perfection!
Pregnant with progression!
Peep the progress.
Never interrupt God while birth is in the process!
God planted this gift in me,
so I'm gonna reap the harvest!
Hinderances be trying to hold me back
like a harness, but I got heart!
And they say the heart is the hardest muscle.
So with a name like K-Love
You can bet I got the hardest hustle!

They couldn't stop my flow
even if they locked my jaw
with the hardest muzzle.
I'll break free,
like cars with no pads.
just me, God and my notepad,
And I'm writing the vision,
and making it clear.
I speak life over my life
and I spit death to kill fear.
Only room for building here,
like the Sears tower.
Tapping into serious power,
and it's only just begun.
Everyday I wake up and ask myself,
"How could I not be great,
when I was created by the Greatest one?"

<u>Walk In Your Calling</u>

Stop chasing dreams and walk in your calling.

When you are chasing something,

that says that it is running away from you.

Why allow yourself to be out of breath?

When you are walking in your calling,

You move with confidence, assured, purposeful,

knowing you'll reach the goal at hand... No need to

worry or run. It's like breathing...

Chasing a dream instead of walking in your calling

is like going after the person you know doesn't want

you, while ignoring the person that's right in front of

you waiting to be acknowledged.

Don't do your calling like that.

<u>Shrinkage</u>

When you shrink the light of who you are
on a spiritual level just to make
a person you're around feel comfortable,
you are not only doing yourself a disservice,
you are actually doing them a disservice as well.

We ALL have light inside of us;
you hiding yours allows them to
be comfortable with ignoring their own...

You shining yours boldly,
brightly may create uneasy feelings within them,
but it is that discomfort that causes self-evaluation
and reflection which may lead to them realizing that,
they too not only possess their own shine,
but they also have a responsibility
to light the world up...

Anti-Struggle

Grass don't struggle to grow;
sun don't stress to shine.

If something is taking too much
energy to do, that may be a sign
that it's not what you are supposed
to be doing...

There's a time to quit and re-direct your energy.

An Inside Job

Some people look at your glow or walk of purpose
and try to obtain it from the outside in...

Meaning they look and be like,

"Oh, all she did was this? I'm finna do that!"

That's not quite how it works.

You see the outside work it took/takes, but you don't
have a clue of the inside work required.

All the prayers, correction, purging, feelings of
failure, anxiety, humility, the confrontation of
conviction, and internal discord...

Walking in your calling/purpose is an Inside job,
there's nothing surface about it.

If you want the next level,

be ready to go deeper.

Shrinkage
(Continued)

...And further-more, wanting to shrink for
acceptance has a lot to do with a fear of
lack. Like believing you won't get another
mate or a friend if this one leaves,
so you gotta walk on egg shells in who you
are so that they don't go.
As if God ain't made your life
abundant in all areas.

Focus

It takes too much
energy to tear others down,
even if they deserve it.

Every minute you spend throwing
rocks at someone else's Queendom
is a minute you could have been
using to turn those rocks into
bricks to build your own.

Negative energy is distracting,
but focus...

Survivor

Today, I stop giving people
who set out to harm me, credit for teaching me
lessons they never intended to.

I'm notorious for giving people who
tried to hurt me accolades for my ability to find
power in the pain they inflicted.

Because I'm not a malicious person,
it's been very difficult for me to
accept that someone would
actually hurt me on purpose...

Hard to accept that
people do in fact act with ill intent.

Today I celebrate myself for my resilience
in surviving toxic people.

Today I celebrate myself for always
looking for the sugar in the salt.

O-Fences

You ever been offended
into greatness???

A person make you soooo mad,
you mess around and become
amazing on they ass?

Lbvs...

Offenses are fences:
climb over and be great.

Watch Me Work

Watch me work!
Show you why they call me Mother Earth.
I'm down-er than the ground you stand on.
Im hands on.
Hands on hips.
Quick witted.
Quick with it.
Came equipped with it.
Shift wit it,
but I never clock out.
I rock out!
Better than ya trap house.
Better ask bout
She.
The Thrift Store shoppin,
Show stoppin,
Nation building,
Wound healing,
Womb healing
Warm feeling,
With the warm filling,
Suzy Q.
Such a effn lady,
raising ya babies and
Ya I.Q.
Heres a Haiku.
Amen be A man. (5)
But its kinda funny cuz.(7)
Ash'e be A she.(5)

Praise be,
to the Most High.
I see the humor.
Laughin
Rumor has it,
I'll pull ya tailcoat,
On some other sh*t.
I mother sh*t.
The Mother Ship,
I raise you little sail boats!
You can't skip her,
Skipper!
I'm zero no higher.
Angels carry my clouds.
Dudes wanna Mar(r)y Mcloud.
They yearning, for the learning.
My Aura burning.
I shoot the flame at 'em.
I came at em thorough.
Cuz I'm standing on the shoulders
Of Margret Burroughs.
And only a true lion can tame her.
Fannie Lou Hamer.
Never forget who nannied you strangers
They say we endangered.
Say we in danger,
but I say,
We end Danger!
Educated black woman.
I be Like Bat Woman.
The Goddess Gotham.
Got the Gods

up out the gutta
With new linings,
by the daughters water.
I write alkaline.
I'm out the lines.
Try to decipher mine,
It'll be the first time
you get a cypher from a line.
I'm that refined fine.
Like God made me cute twice in one life time.
What's life without a woman's life line?
I manifest.
And I'm fresh.
No need to check fashion week.
I don't fashion the weak.
No need to see who wore it best.
I got that Nzinga demeanor,
I'm war at best!
I'm worth the struggle
it is to keep me.
I'm Phyllis Wheatley.
I go against the grain,
but I'm good for you,
Eat me!
I'm food for thought.
Look what I brought!
I got all these tools.
All theses jewels.
Aldis, Jewels.
Fed all theses dudes
off Aldi's food.
We havin' miracles for dinner.

I'm the resource center that
restores sinners.
Enlightenin, and I'm vital man,
like a vitamin,
wit an Echinecea chaser.
Jackie, Sojouner, Truth
Diva.
Better believe her.
I'm something like a Kathleen Clever.
Dudes on the block,
thought I was a *Thot*
I think not!
I'm Nefertiti, Sweetie,
I'm a good catch...
but ya net too teenie!
I'm Assata and Afeeni Shakur,
And even before that,
I raised more than half of a four pack.
Need more facts?
I done Mothered a plenty a fella.
I'm Winnie Mandella.
Stellar, wit hella grace.
No Biggie...
Just hella Faith!
No one can take my place.
I own it! Period! I'm on it!
So give me my space, Tom.
I was ya first friend.
Before your matter even mattered,
you sat on some woman's bladder...
So why you mad at her?
Give me a hug MAN

I'm Harriet TubMAN!
When you Panther's
were just some little Cubs MAN,
I washed ya White Sox, and put you in the tub MAN!
Where's the love MAN?
What's a man's hand
with out the warmth of a woman's a glove MAN?
When its cold MAN!
You sleepin on me,
but I'm Fly-er than the rest.
No foreal you sleepin on me
but I'm fly-er than the *rest*
I'm just that Betsy ColeMAN!
Watch me work!

"Comprehension Levels"

Somebody said I was
hard to read...

My thoughts:
What's your reading level?

#levelstothis

<u>Organically Weird</u>

Somebody also told me
I was weird, and they
believed that it was an
intentional weird...

Nah Bruh, this weird
is organic asf.

#since1982 #iwokeuplikethis

Lmao

<u>No Duplicates</u>

People can easily do what you do,
but they'll never be able to do it with the passion,
conviction, or diligence with which you do it because
they aren't doing it with the same intentions.

You're doing it because it's your calling.
They're doing it hoping to receive a call.
There's a difference.
Pure energy can't be copied.

What's from the heart surely reaches the heart.

#noduplicates

Put Up

Sometimes what
feels like isolation
Is really protection.
God has you put up.

Unlimited Plan

Even when my
lover won't call me back
My calling, stay calling
Thank God I can call on that...
#Facts

Pee Pee Premonition

You know how when you're coming home from a day
out and have to pee, it seems to intensify the
closer you get to your door?

Like, while you're in the car, you're fine;
going up the stairs, you're cool, but as soon as you're
standing in front of your door, key in hand, you can't
seem to stop yourself from doing the pee pee dance.
You may even start to accept the fact that your grown ass
is going to totally have an "accident."

But at last, you arrive at your pee pee destination, not a
minute too late or too soon. In that moment, the release
doesn't feel any less amazing, even after all the waiting
and fidgeting.

Well see, that's sorta how life is when you are on the
brink of completing a goal. It gets toughest the closer you
get to the finish line.

In those moments, you have to strengthen those
"growing" (groin) muscles... and hold it...

Knowing you WILL make it...

Unless you typically pee on yourself. In that case,
totally disregard this entire post.

24

INTIMID8TING

The men I've dated have stated that my power is intimidating.
They say they think I'm amazing,
What I do with the words and the youth,
Admitted that I'm official but they can't handle the truth.
They say it's dope that I'm standing on my square,
But it makes them feel like the shape that's beneath me when they're not currently standing on theirs...
 and I'm like damn, I get that!
I'm only doing what I can.
6 pack.
Doing what I know.
I'm from the go,
Pursing what I love,
So every second is grind time like I'm dirty winding in Jamaican clubs.
And though I love making love...
I'm starting to think my better half better mask himself as a dope as line or a child that needs attention or I'll miss him,
Or maybe I should settle for a simile or cuddle up with this composition,
Cuz my calling is calling and the calling is so persistent that I can't block her.
She's like a stalker.
Got me walking through the crowd to the stage
when I'd really rather be walking down the aisle to the altar.
But what brother finna be bothered?
Or father the babies I've mothered with no bloodline ties?
Who want a woman so accountable
for so many lives?
Watched by so many eyes.

My purpose is pushy,
And the walls of my love have become numb
waiting for my time to come.
I was 31 when I realized that I can't rhyme me a sun
Or marry a metaphor.
So maybe I'll metamorph...
into a pen, to paper mate.
No matter how much money my pen and paper make,
I can't shake the thoughts of being a wife and motherhood.
I keep wondering if I'll ever be the kind of wife and mother
my mother would be proud of.
And though I love my art form,
I be thinking, Who gon keep my heart warm?
Like maybe I should trade this notepad for a Boaz...
and in between the sheets,
he and I can write my greatest masterpiece,
An umbilical cord connected to a life that feeds through me.
Nothing more beautiful then this fete is.
Nothing more beautiful than this fetus.
And I'll be featured in his or her features.
Sure to be my greatest display of talent,
 but I'm struggling with balance.
Insufficient funds,
No fun.
Leaving me no time
to get some.
A social life,
that's so so light,
because they say my soul is so light
It's blinding!
Breaking my heart man,
Even Steve Baartman said that I was a good catch, bad timing.

Ask the Cubs,
I ain't lion.
I'm overbearing.
So Mufasas'
feel miniscule,
Even when I'm submitting,
they get to tripping,
thinking that the crowd is gonna steal their attention.
Their insecurities
that I attempt to secure and easy,
but to no avail.
Seems like the same thing that attracts brothers
seems to be what makes them repel and rebel.
And yes I'm pretty on the stage from a distance,
but the instance he gets a whiff of what my worth is,
he's hesitant to purchase.
And all of a sudden my true value,
is actually a deterrent.
So no sooner than he waves hi,
he gets concurrent with the currents and waves bye.
And I'm left to cry,
And rely on the mic for a shoulder.
Write in my folder.
Seems like my wreck of a love life
only makes the shi*t I write colder.
And yeah I rock the mic,
but the weight of the wait for my soulmate
is starting to feel like boulders.
Because he likes her,
and he likes her,
and he likes her, but won't wife her.
And the only rings I see coming my way these days are cyphers.

And I see bands,
but they're usually playing behind the open mic-ers.
And it sets in when the sets end.
After intense shows,
my tense shows.
Realizing I'm surrounded
by toads in prince clothes.
Poetic princess,
awaiting her Knight,
And hating it's arrival at the same time.
See a Knight meaning a good man would be just fine.
But the night that time defines,
only reminds,
that it's only me
and these rhymes,
and this movement.
And yeah my tongue is a church for the hurt...
but it gets so lonely in this pulpit.
No bull-sh*t...
I'm far from hopeless,
so of course I get onlookers and approachers that approach
her...
But right then in there I realize I'm some little girl's Oprah,
And she's gonna choose what I showed her.
So when choosing a soldier,
my standards can't be standard.
And I understand it's not an easy job.
I recognize that the Goddess inside me
needs a God,
but it's kinda hard to seize a God,
When the King's I meet look in the mirror
and never even see a God.

Seems like the King's self esteem be so scarred,
so he quits before he even starts.
Sees me and sees an artist...
instead of seeing a heart.
Automatically assuming I need big cribs and cars,
material wealth...
when I'd really do better with a God
of ethereal health.
Someone to heal the healer when he holds her.
Someone to wash her locks
when nation building over loads her.
Someone to free me
when I'm feeling like a prisoner to my purpose.
Vindicate me when I'm feeling like a victim to my verses.
And when superwoman is done saving the
entire world,
It would be nice to have a brother that cradles me
and allows me to be a little girl.
Please don't let the lime light
and the mic
and the passion,
steal a wife and a mother...
still waiting to happen.
Please don't be intimidated.

<u>U</u>napologetically Intimid8ting

I used to really feel bad about being intimidating,
primarily to men, but women as well.

I'd been being labeled this way for years.

It was like I wouldn't even be trying to make anyone
feel any negative way about themselves, but some-
how, something about the way I spoke: my direct-
ness, my gift, my conviction to walk in my calling, or
the respect I required just in presence alone... it all
seemed to make some people feel some type of way.

This used to make me feel so outcast and isolated
knowing that people loved me, but stayed away or
pulled away because of feelings of fear or inadequacy
I unintentionally evoked.

I really wanted to be wanted,
accepted and embraced.

I tried to turn my light off, shut my soul up,
quiet my confidence, act less self aware, spiritually
shrink, and just up the dosage of love I gave those
that I knew were intimidated.

None of that worked.
It only made them find ways to punish me passive aggressively for how my presence made them feel, even when I called myself "minimizing".

Men withheld attention, affection, and/or titles. Women jokingly insulted me or stayed trying to find flaw in who I was.

Very recently, I decided to stop giving a f#?&.

You know why?

I realized that I'm not responsible for how people feel about themselves, especially if I'm not intentionally tearing them down.

I can't carry that weight.
It doesn't belong to me.

Feelings of intimidation can be likened to feelings of discomfort. Discomfort is a main ingredient in the soil of growth.

I realized that the intimidation that I might happen to cause could quite possibly ordain discomfort meant to spark or challenge that person to look inside of themselves in search of their own light.

You Know You Knew

If only we could have total
trust in our spirit, gut, intuition
the FIRST time.

You always know what to do,
even when you say you don't.

Confusion is an illusion.

You know, you knew.

Walls

As a free spirit,
the hardest lesson
I've had to learn is the
necessity of building walls.

It's vital to the
preservation of
this big heart.

Spiritual Stacks

Nah... I ain't got the
money you got,
but you ain't got
the spirit I got either...

Can I Get A Refill

Don't stroke my ego; feed my spirit.
Bringing the water to the people
often leaves me drained and empty.

Any brother I'm gonna be with
have to know how to refill
the vessel from a spiritual aspect.

GPS

Here's the thing with a GPS...

Unless you change the destination,
you will end up right where you left.
It may give you
an alternate route. You can take that route,
make all the turns and twists on it,
and really begin to feel like you're
going somewhere else.
You may even pass
landmarks you've never seen, but guess what?
When you park the car again, you will
undoubtedly be back in the same damn spot.

Lesson here: Before you pull off,
make sure you've changed your destination.

Trap Anointing

Aye look, don't be surprised to see me
ANYWHERE! I'm a spirit.God energy.
I'm everywhere God is....

The block
The church
Colleges
The club
The crib
The corner
The mosque
Yo mama nem house...

I'm in the cut shining my light.

I go where God sends me
And I'm always right at home

#arealperson
#dontgetittwisted
#ilovemypeople

Poster Girl

Reflections

Reflections

Reflections

Reflections

Reflections

Reflections

Reflections

Reflections

What She's Wearing

Teach Me How To Give Up

Teach me how to give up.
Show me how to surrender.
Convey to me the way to concede
to my contenders,
cuz as long as I can remember,
I've been fighting,
feet firmly planted battle grounds,
bucking, even when I'm out of rounds.
I'm still in the ring, going through the ringer
Ike and Tina
Joe Jackson, thrashin
Bobbin and weavin
Like Yaki low in the back wit the sides even.
Even when I'm tired, I don't know treason.
Show me how to bring the trees in.
Show me how to branch off from something
I Be LEAVE in.
What's leaving? I've never done it before.
I was the muse Sun Tzo used for the Art of war.
I never quit, even when I should.
I'm no good at giving up,
a philanthropist when it comes to given a F&$#,
I give so many.
It's the soul in me.
heart of gold in me,
I never harbor the heart breaks.
I'm hard to break.
Peer pressured by my faith,
It be in my face, like *That's all you can take?*
Now I'm feeling like a petty thief,

Provoking me prolong the pain.

I stay in the game, even when I'm getting played.

I don't know how to give.

Steadfast,

The only way I know how to live.

Maybe my faith got a big ego.

Don't know how to let go of people,

Like my palms sweat super glue,

Scared to loose and lose.

I wanna master good byes,

But I spend too much...time.

Afraid to plant a seed and turn my back and miss the tree it could grow to be.

My optimism be on over-drive.

Got me tired of being tied to my ties.

Dedication is doomed to be my demise.

Cuz I don't know how to quit.

I go in hard like hallow tips.

Only allow my all to all of it.

Always on some self martyr sh*#

Wishing I woulda never started it.

I get tense and intense when I feel it started to slip,

Then I'm back reloading the clip and I'm bucking again,

Like F@&# it...I'm in!

I do it to the death.

Give my total best

Even when there's no more left.

Giving plenty,

Even when I'm empty.

Ask my past men or any if my mentees.

I don't know how not to be committed.

Feeling like I should be committed

Poster Girl

To the psych ward
Married to monogamy,
Even when they doggin me.
I keep showing up,
even when I'm sick & throwing up
I never abort the mission.
I'm totally vested in the vision.
My every intention is to see things thru,
Believing in you when you can't even convince you too.
So what do I do in this cold world?
Where reciprocity is obviously an oddity,
Where the masses are average,
Would rather half-ass it,
A haphazard,
My friends seem to favor fragments.
Leaving me feeling like
A run in sentence
In a book of
Incomplete thoughts,
An extended metaphor
In an highschool of hykus.
I'm looking at all these fools who like to lose
And I refuse to.
Feelng like I'm in a *Do better* desert,
Unworthy endeavors
Not worth the effort,
And I'm like a broke GPS...
I dont know the way to go.
And though I know who
I a.m.
Don't how to say F.m.
Radio,

Don't teach me how to dougie, nah,
Teach me how to give up...
when I've got every reason to...
When I'm surrounded by people who
Treat me like an electrical socket.
Draining my juice,
Slicing my fruit,
Ninjas disrespecting my truth,
Still giving me pebbles when you know how hard I've been rocking with you.
Im not usually one for exposing who I do,
but yes it's true, I do...
too much,
and occasionally I ménage wit The Most
Now I'm pregnant with expectations
And most folks can't even seem cum close...
And its my fault.
I'm over top,
Roller coaster,
How am I suppose to stop,
When I was born a rider...
Self proclaimed survivor,
So I'm often intrigued by the trials,
Often in the denial bout when it's time to detach, I relapse and reboot,
re-loop my noose, call me a self masseuse
I be holding me back,
See thats my gift and my curse,
I do it like the God I serve.
Pursue with intentions of permanent positions,
Half jobs be absurd.
I pride myself on resilence,

But maybe I've been building to fall,
Giving too much when they can't handle it all.
Maybe I'm too loose with my dilligence...
I do diligence
Even when it's not due diligence...
I'm still in it.
Going hard like I put steel in it.
Even when its un-deserved,
I serve.
Leaving me under served
Like an unhappy customer,
I get everybodys sloppy copies
While they get a custom her,
That should have been preserved,
Until earned,
Because the ashes,
of unappreciated actions,
Will always leave you burned.
So maybe I don't need to learn how to give up,
I just need to better discern...
Who to give up on.

Laundry Or Lesson?

If you pay attention..You can further learn
yourself in the smallest instances..

Example: I did laundry last night..After putting my
last load in the dryer I closed the door and loaded
the quarters. $1.50...quarters right? So after putting
in my 5th one, the machine i was using stopped regis-
tering my quarters. I put 1 more quarter in to see if it
would change, nope. I said well maybe it tweaked for
a second, let me add another one. NOPE. I waited a
few minutes and said ok maybe now it has reset itself
and I added yet another one. Noooooope. I added
5 extra quarters to a machine that showed me that it
wasn't working a whole 6 or quarters ago.

Were there other machines there? Absolutely. For
whatever reason, I had faith in that one. Probably
because my clothes were wet, heavy and already in
there. I figured it made more sense to stick with that
particular machine since I had already put $1.25 in
and all that was needed was for it to take one more
quarter. I couldn't accept the fact that I obviously
couldn't make it take said quarter.

Needless to say the clothes are still not dry...
and I have to now journey to
get more change for a new machine.

As a result, I cant wear what I wanted to today, because I wasted time and energy on a broken machine.
SMH, convenience will cost you something too...

LESSON:
This scenario is indicative of areas in my life. I tend
to have faith in things that i know aren't working
properly and rather than investing in something new,
I continue to invest in the old for reasons of convenience, believing that I'm saving time and energy
when I'm really losing both..

Realization is the first step to change..

Know what to give up on... #MESSAGE

Simone's Scripture

It's ok to accept and date people who are
"works-in-progress" (aren't we all)

but remember,
there are levels to progress...

and some levels of progress are not
acceptable for entering
into relationships.

That's a word...

The Gift Of Ghosting

Sometimes what feels like
rejection is actually
high respect and great regard.

The brother ain't wanna waste your time,
he knew better than even you did
that you were worthy of a certain
quality of experience that he knew
he wasn't prepared to give you...

His ghosting was a gift.

Cheat Sheet Freak

Some people aren't really interested
in building with you, but rather
building themselves off you.

They only want to stand *beside* you.

Though they look up to you,
you have been mis-purposed in
their lives as a stepping stool.

Your presence serves as a cheat sheet
for how to be, have, or obtain
the light that they envy.

They can't clap for you when
they are too busy taking notes
on how to become you.

Fake Love

There are people that I'll share laughs with,
but never share my dreams or future goals with...

Because underneath their
funny jokes, their souls are
soaked in jealousy and envy

And though
my flesh is entertained and
amused by their humor.
My spirit is a gangsta,
serving them the stale
face the whole time.

#discernmentonfleek

Accountable Integrity Deficiency

Things brothers have told me
that make me go "Hmm..."

One dude:
"With you, I hate talking to you because
I know I'm going to be held
accountable for every word I say."

Another brother said:
"I have to think too much
before I say things to you."

Another brother said:
"I'm usually kinda mean and careless with how I
speak to other women, but for some reason,
I can't seem to do that with you."

Like, wtf???

Should I feel bad about requiring
a brother to use thought, consideration, and accountability when conversing with me?

Poster Girl

Like, should you not be accountable
for what you say?

Should you not have to think before speaking?
Should you be able to just talk reckless to me?

I'm glad you know better.

Know Your Role

You can't love feelings of
inadequacy out of a person.
If you're intimidating to a person,
there's nothing you can do
to be less intimidating.
The only thing that person can do
is decide to become more confident.

Cellular Man

I call him my cellular man,
with the TRACK PHONE plan.
He wanna keep contact,
with no CONTRACT.
He figures no TERMS, no violation,
just incase'n
he wanna ROAM
like his phone's in a bad location.
He wanna be free on the OUT-GOING,
and IN-COMING
for whenever he feel like coming in.
And I'm like... Hold up! Come again?!
You want an UNLIMITED PLAN
but you got limited plans,
MR. TELEPHONE man!
Wanna come over and roll over in it,
with no ROLL-OVER MINUTES.
Wanna be mobile
on his T-MOBILE so he can SPRINT to the NEXTEL,
and if that fails,
he think he gon have me on CALL-WAITING to exhale,
but I ain't Whitney,
so I'm like hell to the naw,
bout to mess around and miss yo call.
I don't wanna tie up his lines.
He said he needed space
so I gave him a GALAXY times 5.
He steady swearing that a change gon come,
but gettin sick of him
singing the same song that SAM-SUNG.
I just about done.

had him programmed in my cell under
HUBBY,
We got matching *smart* phones
but he still wanna be a dummy!
And I used to do him real right,
Let him in the space that holds life
but tonight he got his buds all in his ear
so I told him, good luck wit his HAND-held device.
My conversation gonna be shorter
than ANDROID battery life.
I'm finna to the left him.
No replies when I'm TEXTING?
That's ok, I know guys that think I'm fly,
steady tryin to SWIPE, like KEYBOARD settings,
And I'm gonna let em!
But he say I'm insecure,
And he swear he aint like me,
but he steady trying to SKYPE me.
All up in my CONTACTS,
trying to see who I'm seeing.
Wanna play me on the down low,
I told him to kiss my APPS if he don't wanna download.
But, he think he got me whipped
 like he carry a switch
I doubt that.
Don't lack.
Mess around get yo CARRIER switched.
Cuz my exes still love my BLACK BERRY,
and wanna marry a Miss.
My juice is still sweeter than the rest,
That's why I keep it on the CHARGER.
I'm at 100 percent,

Poster Girl

I told him to keep his energy,
don't even bother.
God even tried to send him a message.
I thought he would of have seen that,
but his SCREEN cracked.
I even got my phone giving him the SILENT
treament,
Get this...
I can't hear him
With no RING!
(Points to ring finger)
Know what I mean?
So it's like I cut it off.
Switched it over to the VIBRATOR.
Said "Call me back!"
Maybe we could vibe later.
But for now I just got tired of the lying.
I said what's up with your LINE?
Maybe you should check it.
Sorry, what I meant to say is,
The number you have reached has been...
Disconnected!

Clear Water

Your words and actions must
be specific and clearly defined.

If you're trying to date me, you gotta say that.
If you need me to mentor you, you gotta say that.
If you want to build a friendship,
you gotta say that.

And after that's been clearly stated, let's set
boundaries and stay in the lanes we've designed.

All else will breed confusion.

I'm not reading between lines or guessing.

You gotta be mature enough to
say what you want flat out.

All CLEAR water over here

#Im35 #Grownasf

Prepare A Place For Me

I only desire to go where a place
has been prepared for me.
I have no desire to force my
way or fit into a space.

If you want me there, make room.

<u>Worthy</u>

I'm not naive;
I just really believe that
I'm deserving of miracles.
So yeah, in my life, I've bought
a few of the dreams brothers
were selling; not solely because I had
faith in them, but because I knew I was
worthy of what was being proposed,
no matter how far out it was.

And even though they didn't always deliver...

I STILL believe I'm worth
a brother attempting to do the impossible.

A Fathers Affirmation

My Daddy just liked my pic on Facebook.
It reminded me of how much his affirmation
meant to me as a child.

My mother would want to comb my
hair and I'd be crying, whining and fussing
and my Daddy would be like...
"Come on cry-baby, let mommy make
Daddy's baby pretty." When she'd get
done he'd make a big deal about it.

"Ohhhh look that's Daddy's pretty baby
right there!" Men, affirm your daughters
while their young. Give them your words.
Tell them how smart, beautiful,
and talented they are. It'll help to shape them
into powerful, confident, women.

Mama's Gift

My mother tells me
that I am a gift.

Gifts never force themselves on
people. They don't have to,
they're GIFTS!?!!

And if a person can't recognize
or doesn't feel worthy enough
to accept the gift, it's surely not the gift's
responsibility to convince
them to take the gift.

<u>Worth It</u>

Sis, if you are a good woman and you know your worth, then you know that you are worth a brother:

Forgiving you · Adjusting for you
Considering you · Fighting for you
About you · Beside you · Learning you
Believing you · Having faith in you
Trusting you · Giving you another chance
Respecting you · Making you a priority
Giving you his heart · Sharing his time with you
Claiming you · Being patient with you
Waiting for you · Protecting you · Accepting you.

Don't feel bad about requiring any of these things from a brother you're sharing your soul, spirit, and body with... These are more than reasonable requests from a brother who says that he wants you...

Especially if you're giving him
all that's mentioned as well.

You are worth reciprocity.
Have a requirement.

#lessons

Cape Off

I love people who know
I'm superhuman,
but still allow me to
be super human.

Loveless Self

Loving someone
more than you love
yourself sounds beautiful...
but it's not love at all...
It's beautiful self-hatred...
An ugly cut with a
pretty band-aid.

Reflections

Reflections

Reflections

Reflections

Reflections

Reflections

Reflections

Reflections

The Height Of Her Heel-ing

Journey to Self Love

You too grown to be getting played girl.
Still trying to make a family tree.
Still coming up with shade, girl.
I thought I told you,
Lemons alone can't make no lemonade, girl.
Why you crying over milk spilled in a pitty war?
What you think you got them titties for?
You made the man and the milk he drinks,
so what makes you think
you won't have enough?
Why are you so thirsty?
Beggin simp for a sip when you cuffin D cups.
Its been written;
Every Goddess shall be made with double d's.
Spell-check, Queen, please.
How you starvin for affection, when u feed the block on the
daily?
You out here mothering thugs and rocking babies.
What you look like,
"The giver of life,"
dying for attention,
being perceived as the
needy type?
That ain't right.
Like a trail left of broke pens,
thats cray cray hun,
so I grabbed a Sharpie,
to write A letter to you,
And it starts out,
"Dear self,

How these dudes know
the power in your womb
better than you?"
Are you a Visionary with no sight?
Blind to own light?
Raving bout their rays,
when daily you and the sun skype.
One night your gonna wake up
and realize that throne
you've been sitting on
all this time.
You've been preaching to you
Through you in all these rhymes
Thinking your gift is where their presence is,
meanwhile it's been living in your residence.
When you gon love YOU like you love
HIM?
When you gon realize
You can't turn a *Hope* into a *Husband!*
When you gone practice what you preach?
You doing acrobatics in these sheets
for a ghost of a guy you can't even keep.
When you gon choose you?
Stop letting thoughts of a wedding noose you!
See what happens when finding a mate
consumes you?
You'll mess around and find him and lose you,
but that's just food for thought,
only If you choose to chew.
Choose the truth.
Why you treating your castle
like a shack?

Rebounding with rebounds.
Bring yo boundaries back!
Put yo back bone back on Sally Walker!
even if it means walking alone...
You out here looking real grown,
Talking bout where yo heels at...
knowing you ain't healed yet.
You might wanna pull out your comfy shoes...
And pack light,
Plenty of it.
You're gonna need it.
And yes, the lonely monster will come,
but I promise, you will not be defeated.
And I know you've been lied to,
cheated.
You've been the mistress,
the main chick,
the vixen, the bang chick
and even the naive dip.
You've compromised to nurse woes,
agreed to being one of his 3 hoes.
Justified it to yourself by saying "Well atleast I know!"
And you do...
You know that you deserve more
than his residue.
He's exactly where he wants to be,
why you steady trying to rescue dude?
You aint "Captin save a hoe!"
That's not your character!
Acknowledge that you played the role!
And It's ok.
Because we've all been type-casted,

Given up our own existence for someone else,
putting our actual self in a casket.
Need our ass kicked,
for acting so passive in passion,
practically asking for death.
But only you can speak life to yourself.
On those nights to yourself...
Wonder why they left you alone,
when you were never right to yourself.
Sometimes you gotta write to yourself.
You hold that right to yourself.
Grab up all your goodies & goodness
And give em right to *yourself.*
What you're looking for...
you won't find it in no one else.
There's no greater power than to know one's self.
So do your research.
Find the orgin of each hurt.
Trace it's path.
You might need to fast.
Take a spiritual bath.
Get some tea-tree and lemon grass.
Burn some white sage.
Place a candle on your mantle and let the fire flicker and fade.
Get in the water,
Place your hands on your womb
And meditate.
Breathe...with both hands
in a pyramid on the center of self,
center yourself.
Send for your self esteem.
Dig up your dignity.

Summon your strength.

You'll find some in your strength.

Do some chakra aligning.

You'll be shocked with the findings.

And you'll find you'll be arriving

with perfect timing,

never minding,

the time you've been wasting.

Forgive yourself.

Be patient with yourself.

Remind yourself,

that Self love is a *journey*,

Never a destination.

Self Surgery

It's easier to hear that you're not
enough than to hear that you're too much.
If you're not enough you can add things
to who you are, but if you're too much,
you have to cut parts of you off.
That's painful.

<u>Still Bleeding</u>

If you sit still and quiet long enough,
you may find that some of the wounds that you
thought were now scars are actually still wounds,
still bleeding and in need of some care.

Just because you think that you
should be over it, doesn't
mean you're over it.

Healing has no respect for time frames.

It's takes as long as it takes and
that time is tripled when you choose to
ignore the fact that you're still hurt.

I'm not suggesting wallowing in that pain,
I'm suggesting acknowledging it and treating
yourself with care until it's fully healed..

Pain Pals

Some people are in love with their pain.
Happiness is a choice you have to choose daily.

Life will never be perfect but if we
choose to focus on the perfect moments within it,
we'll get more of those moments.

But I legit believe some people like
being depressed. It gives them
something to hold on to.

Choose happiness.
Amplify your good days and good moments

<u>Closure</u>

Stop waiting on people to
give YOU *closure*.

You better grab a needle
and some thread and
get yo stitch game up!

#theydontloveyoulikeyoushould

Forgive Yourself

NEVER let others hold you
in bondage to their forgiveness.

Sincerely apologize if you
feel in your spirit that you were wrong,
but whether they accept your apology or not,
that's on them. Move on.

Liquid Love

People tell you to love yourself
all the time like it's that easy..

Sometimes, by way of bad experiences
and self hatred, we find ourselves so
far away from it that where to start
can be confusing ...and that's ok

If you don't know where to
begin on the journey of loving yourself

Start by drinking more water.
Imagine that each glass is
liquid love you are pouring into yourself.

Remi-Riyah

I cried for you yesterday,
as I pressed play on your reality
Soundbites of
slaughters
sanity
soiled sanitary napkins
Noises of the news
of your noose
on the net
Nothing nastier than that,
attempting to show how dirty you were,
while filming in filth,
She stinks at motherhood...
Where do you run when mommy
is the monster under your bed?
in your head,
when your demons are how her face looks
Nightmare on Facebook
Bags of dirty laundry
Aired like reruns
Of dysfunctional family matters
featuring
pathetic parenting
Worse than Monique in that movie
treated like Precious
a diamond as ruby
I wished she knew you were precious
That puberty already feels like prison

to little girls, pimples and periods, sentenced and chained in the
changes they can't control
Like slaves
trying to master
Illiterate bastard!
plastered to ears
Belittling you
Dumb woman
with a smart phone
Destroying her home
I could have sworn I saw the camera cry
during your crucifixion
Time stood paralyzed on my time line
your eyes
terrified
Searching
lens for mercy,
hurting, eyes
waving white flags
saying I surrender,
screaming uncle!!!
Where was your Dad ?
Fantasy of a father?
The super hero in your dreams who
always came to stop her,
Maybe she'd already murdered him
with the same mouth
Emasculated crumbs of his pride swept under the couch
Maybe he died when he entered her...

<u>Random Thoughts On Sex</u>

How do you get rid of the demons
that sex with the wrong person,
at the wrong time, left you with?

Well, here are a few methods I have used:

1. Fasting: abstaining from a certain
thing for a certain amount of days,
and filling the time that you'd
usually engage in that thing with prayer.

You may need to abstain from
that person. Give yourself 21 days of no
communication in any way (not to hurt
them because even if you received bad energies from
intimacy with them, it doesn't mean they're a
terrible person). Fast from them to build
up a spiritual resistance that helps
stabilize your emotions.

2. Writing affirmations that affirm
better decision making, discernment,
and forgiveness for self on note cards.

Post them all around your crib,
especially in your bedroom.
Carry them around with you.
Periodically, look at them.
Recite them to yourself
every time you think of it.

3. Journal or vent to a friend.

Openly and honestly speak or write about
what you did, how it felt, etc.
BE BLUNT. CRY if you need to.
Make sure that after getting it all out,
you write or speak about how you'd
like to feel moving forward.

4. Taking spiritual baths with oil(s)
that help to soothe and calm,
placing hands on your sacred parts
and asking for a release of bad
energies that you knowingly or
unknowingly invited...

Even if you are showering,
every time you touch *there*,
say a prayer asking to be cleansed.

5. Drink lots of water.

Remind yourself that water heals, cleanses,
and is powerful. Write affirmations
of this on the bottle. Believe that it's
working to help you to release.

I don't know everything;
all I know is what I've tried,
and what helped me...

I hope this helps others.

Survivor

I'm a survivor.
You can taste the strength
in my saliva.
I spit fire cause I been through it.
Call me Sister struggle,
you can say I'm kin to it.
My Granny was a gangsta.
Diabetes couldn't beat her.
My mama woke up out an 18 hour coma and she still one of the
coldest divas.
Yeah I come from a long line
of wise wives and made men,
who manipulated their way
through the maze
and it made them amazing.
So I follow suit,
like I'm chasing a blazer
or a pair of slacks.
When life's a b!&$@ that bites,
I BITE BACK!
Get whooped enough,
you learn how to put your dukes up
and FIGHT BACK!
So you can call me
the karate chiropractor,
never letting what I lack be a factor.
Reality is determined by the thoughts one has,
so I change my state of mind
more than infants with diaper rash.
I'm not a product of my past,
more like a figment of my future.

I use my setbacks as the suture.

I already know having my heart in pieces only produced some of my hardest pieces.

I've found piece in my pain,

only used it as personal gain.

I read the biblical verse that said, "*Let patience have its perfect work...*" (James 1:4)

So I created it, it's dream job in me.

I had a dream God and me got intimate,

and he told me he ain't into quick,

nor easy, and that the fight's not finished.

He told me in order to be a star starter,

I had to see some benches.

So yes, sister soldier done warred

in some wars,

but I found tenacity in my trenches.

And yes, I got some battle wounds

that hurt like battered wombs

of rape victims,

But I heal quick

like we'll trained pits.

Sustain and maintain when the pain hits.

Picture my picture as I paint it.

You name it, I've seen it,

if not in the physical,

you can bet I've fought them same demons in my mind.

My flesh be trying to test,

but my spirit is a thug whole time.

I'm a renegade at Soul,

worth Oprah Winfrey's weight in gold.

My faith is bold.

There's nothing I can't handle.

Poster Girl

My lights get cut off, I cop candles.
I get down but don't stay down.
My car break down I go Greyhound.
I keep a bus card on deck.
No cash no sweat.
I've never seen a day of my needs not being met.
I'm a vet to adversity.
A pro at problems,
A math whiz at this.
The way I handle hard times
would puzzle Einstein.
I decided, you gotta get tired if crying.
You can either lie down and let life whoop you bad
or you can get swoll and enroll in a Tae Bo class
or something...
And I know your troubles steady coming,
like a revolving door,
and you're tired
like the latest commercial rappers
on your radio,
cause lately yo
bills been body building.
Stress been taking steroids,
seems like your pain gangbangs
and hangs with a posse of poverty,
and you're probably...
praying for a break through
right now as you read,
so I hope you get peace from this piece
that I wrote for the weak.
Let "*There's hope!*" be your quote for the week.
It's all about how you think.

Right now,
 you could start to feel your failures and disappointments be-
neath your feet.
And even if you woke up,
broke up,
YOU STILL WOKE UP!
That says something about you!
Only let this world and its woes
bring that warrior up out you!
You too are a survivor.
You got God's DNA all up in you.
So even when this world tries to break you,
never let it bend you!
You're blessed for what you've been through.
Learn how to let your burdens build you!
In this life keep telling yourself,
*"The only things that can make you stronger, are those things that do
not kill you!"*
You too are a survivor,
and me and God think it's time...
you start acting like it!

<u>Still Fly</u>

Performing with a broken
heart is like a bird flying
with a broken wing.

The shit is difficult...

but the fact that I've done it / I'm doing it,
reminds me of the magic I really am.

Got Light

Question:
Who is pouring light into your soul?

Like, who in your life is feeding you life?

Good food? Healthy thoughts?
Positive affirmations?
Godly conversations?
Sharing Creative ideas?
Encouraging your dreams?
Using kindness to correct you?

We tend to have more than enough people feeding
us b.s. and pleasuring our lower selves.

Zone in on who is bringing you LIGHT!

Spiritual Bath

Baptize yourself in the water; you have
the power to make a regular bath a
holy experience. It's about intention.

While in the tub, talk to God on purpose!
Create intimacy with Creator. Set the mood,
get your candles,crystals, music, and
whatever else you deem to be
holy or of a high spiritual vibration.

After chilling and soaking, when you start to wash,
pray for every part of you that the water touches.
Ask that every cell, organ, etc. function in
the excellence of the Most High.

Now, as you are stepping out of the water,
ask that you be reborn. That everything that didn't
belong in your spirit, mind, and body be left in the
tub to go down the drain.

Finally, believe that it has been done.
Repeat as necessary.
I bet you begin to feel better...
Ask me how I know.

Fall Fasting

These quiet moments this last month
have been some of the most powerful moments
I've ever experienced in my life.

It's like I **KNOW** they are purposed
and I **KNOW** just what to do while I'm in them.

I've done my best reflecting and praying
for parts of myself I may not have realized were
broken while in the noise of life or relationships.
I've been searching every corner of my mind,
heart, and spirit for hidden pain, and intentionally
touching it with love and concern.

I am becoming a different kind of healed, a different
kind of whole that I haven't been.

Affirmative Prayer

Today I feel Powerful. I continue to have that power affirmed everywhere I go. People feel a divine energy that radiates from me. My Goddess swag is in full effect. My touch is healing to all who embrace me; there's no denying that.

My touch is healing to my own temple. Every time I lay my hands on myself, I heal and correct all that's inside of me. I have the wisdom and will power to heal any dis-ease that attempts to attack. I know exactly what to do to manifest my healing and everyday, I learn more. My healthy ways are now my lifestyle. My temple is being prepared to bring forth a child, and I can do it...effortlessly.

All things work out for my good. I bring forth miraculous happenings, medical miracles, and spiritual divinity. My husband-to-be is safe inside of me. He is already waiting for me. He's been specially prepared to love and accept all that is me. I am free of any soul ties that are unhealthy. I have no desire for anything that doesn't naturally gravitate towards me. I spend my energy healing and attracting righteous love.

I release all that is unhealthy mentally, spiritually, emotionally and physically. I embrace true love, righteous love. I embrace forgiveness, clarity, and understanding. I know just what to do in all situations.

I release confusion, and I embrace surety, confidence, and power. Thank you, CREATOR, for filling me with love that attracts more love.

Thank you for mercy, forgiveness, healing, light, direction, and fearlessness.

Ase Ase Ase.

<u>Decide</u>

Stop being afraid to make a decision.

We have to treat our decisions like our children.

Accept them. Wrong or right, you created them.

They are a part of you and apart of your story

Letting Go

Giving up old ideas and
allowing fresh ones to grow...

God will blow your mind with
new thoughts, ideas, relationships,
opportunities, understandings,...

But you may have to let go of
what you thought a thing was supposed to be.

<u>Open Up</u>

When you know it's good for you, good to you...
If it moves you, allow it to move you.
Don't fight against the change.
It's like denying your spirit.
You want the next level of life, right?
Allow it to happen.
Open up...

Empathy, Faith and Optimism

Most of the problems or pain that I've encountered
or suffered came as no surprise to me...

I am, and have always been, very spiritually intuitive
so more times than not, I've foreseen and/or been
urged in my spirit to leave or disconnect from
potentially heart-hazardous situations
before they ever brought harm.

The Problem:

My gift of empathy tends to override my spiritual
intuitiveness and even my love for self at times.

I've stayed in friendships and relationships knowing
they'd lead to my detriment solely because I didn't
want to hurt the other person with my absence.

In true empath fashion, I'd internalize how it would
make them feel, and the pain I thought they would
feel would make me stay.

I'd then use my gifts of faith and optimism to
rationalize why it was ok to stay.

Before I knew it, I'd be back totally committed to things I should have let go, long ago.

#learning

Keep the Change

Hold on to the good moments of life...

Collect them like random change you find
in the cushions of your couches and at
the bottom of old purses.

Put them in the jar of your mind.
They will come through
swhen you need them the most.

I Feel Good

I feel good!
Like a master masseuse,
Like I'm mastering truth,
And my path be the proof.
Like I'm brightest the light in the room,
despite any gloom
I feel like there's no mountain
too mighty to move.
Like I dipped in the fountain of youth.
Like everything I thought I lost,
I found in my youth!
And I declare;
Nothing's gonna ruin my day!
Renewed my faith.
Haters try till they're blue in the face,
but I don't bother with them smurfs,
I'm smirking and smile'n today!
I got every reason to,
been through the storm,
so the season's due.
I believe in who
I see in the mirror,
and I'm seeing her clearer,
with each moment that passes.
I'm feeling fantastic!
I got immaculate health!
I'm alkalined in the mind.
Watered in wealth.
I'm 30 something, & my body still looking right!
Knock out! Hooking right!

With a Goddess looking light.
Booking flights to my destiny.
Got a few riders next to me.
And she woke up like that,
But I woke up!
That's enough!
Breathing on my own!
After a good night, of rocking a mic
I woke up in a bed, sleeping in a home.
And my apartment might be tiny,
but it's where I go to find me.
And I'm finding that matter don't matter
 if the space don't feel safe and sacred.
I know that I'm worthy of mansions,
but give me a closet,
And I bet I'll make it a sanctuary of tranquil.
I'm thankful!
The Ancestors still handing me gems.
I still got the use of my limbs.
Sense in my senses.
Sun still giving me kisses.
Aligned in my chakras,
writing for my life and I'm a hell of an author!
Who da hell gonna stop her?
I got a litany of lyrics,
A borage of bars,
A surplus of spirit,
with a humongous heart...
and Im intune with my God.
Using my art with a purpose,
far from perfect,
but I own it!

Nina Simone it..
in this moment,
I just feel GOOD!
I'm feel loved and protected,
admired, respected,
considered, creative,
artsy, eclectic,
forgiven,
redeemed.
Im living my dream!
Affirming the power that I know is in my bloodstream!
And Yes, at times I've had to stomach hurts,
but I also had some days where Im laughing
till my stomach hurts!
Smiling despite it all.
I got the peace of God and strength to fight it off.
So I get lost...
in a righteous state of mind.
Trying to right this state of mine.
So I write THIS state of mind.
Because it's so easy to speak bout your pain,
so easy to rhyme in rain.
It's easy to put pen to paper
to talk about haters.
But but I say one time
for Sunshine.
She deserves a round of applause.
She's more than a reason to pause,
and get lost in the gratitude of right now.
I wake up every day like, Wow!
I got another day up out this life,
and I didn't have to beg God for a breath.

My mother still alive and healthy
waking up just to pray for me on her steps.
I know I'm blessed!
Even when doubt tries to seep in,
I know my gift still making room for me
like it works for housekeeping.
I know I was made in the image of God,
thats why I'm still winning
even when Im scrimmaging odds.
I just write it all down,
invite a crowd,
and tell my story to the hood.
Im out here prayed up,
I feel way up,
I called my bro J up like...
"Yo Today, I just feel good!"

Poster Girl

Reflections

Reflections

Reflections

Reflections

Reflections

Reflections

Reflections

Reflections

Acknowledgements

I'd like to acknowledge
My parents; Kenneth and Tammy Harris,
My grandparents; Raymond and Judith Harris
My brother; Kenny Harris

My Mentors;
Deana Dean, Prophet Malaak &Yahdna
My Sun and Daughter Mentees;
Courvosier Randolph and Crystal Jones
The Chicago poetry community at large,
Thank you all for believing in me.

Special acknowledgements
My Friend and Photographer; Tony Cash
To my homegirl; Passion NoLastNecessary
for help with editing
To my unofficial team;
Janice Harris, Joey Callahan and Iris Cooley
I'm so grateful.

bookklovepoetry@gmail.com
kloveproducts@gmail.com
@klovethepoet (instagram)